The Classical Piano Method

Christmas Collection

Hans-Günter Heumann

ED 13651

www.schott-music.com

Mainz · London · Madrid · New York · Paris · Prague · Tokyo · Toronto
© 2013 SCHOTT MUSIC GmbH & Co. KG, Mainz · Printed in Germany

ED 13651
British Library Cataloguing-in-Publication Data.
A catalogue record for this book is available from
the British Library
ISMN 979-0-2201-3437-1
ISBN 978-1-84761-331-8

Cover design by www.adamhaystudio.com
Cover photography: iStockphoto

Music setting and page layout by Wega Verlag GmbH
Printed in Germany S&Co.8953

CONTENTS

1. Jolly Old Saint Nicholas

Traditional Christmas Song
Arr.: Hans-Günter Heumann

Accompaniment With accompaniment, student plays one octave higher than written.

2. We Wish You a Merry Christmas

Traditional carol from England, 16th century
Arr.: Hans-Günter Heumann

Fine

D.C. al Fine

Accompaniment   With accompaniment, student plays one octave higher than written.

Fine

D.C. al Fine

3. O Come, All Ye Faithful

Adeste fideles

Text and Music by John Francis Wade (1711–1786)
English text by Frederick Oakeley (1802–1880)
Arr.: Hans-Günter Heumann

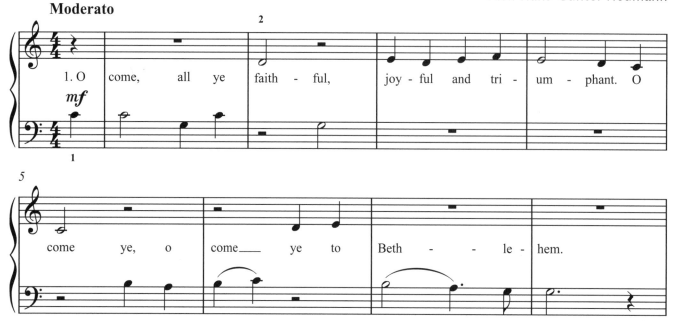

Accompaniment With accompaniment, student plays one octave higher than written.

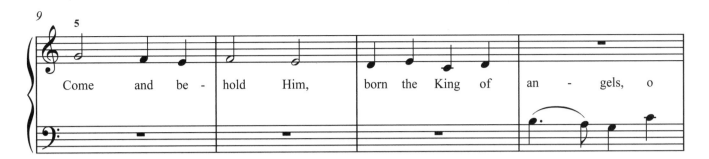

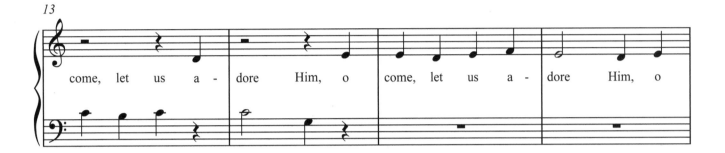

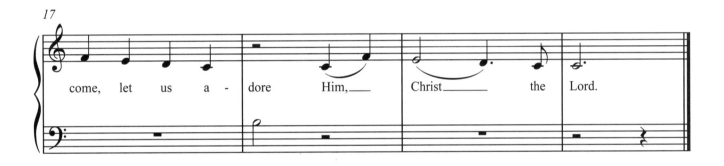

2. Sing choirs of angels,
   sing in exaltation,
   sing, all ye citizens of heaven above;
   Glory to God, in the highest glory,
   o come, let us adore Him,
   o come, let us adore Him,
   o come, let us adore Him,
   Christ, the Lord.

3. Yea, Lord, we greet Thee,
   born this happy morning,
   Jesus, to thee be all glory given;
   Word of the Father now in flesh appearing,
   o come, let us adore Him,
   o come let us adore Him,
   o come, let us adore Him,
   Christ, the Lord.

4. Jingle Bells

The One Horse Open Sleigh

James Lord Pierpont (1822–1893)
Arr.: Hans-Günter Heumann

1. Dash - ing through the snow, in a one horse o - pen sleigh, o'er the fields we go laugh - ing all the way. Bells on bob - tail ring, they're mak - ing spir - its bright, what fun it is to ride and sing a sleigh - ing song to - night! Oh!

*) Don't play the small notes in the left hand if the accompaniment part is also present.

Accompaniment With accompaniment, student plays one octave higher than written.

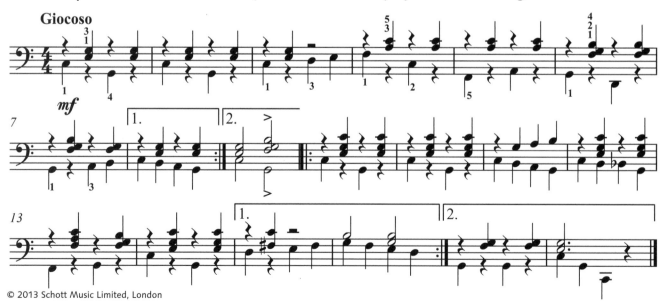

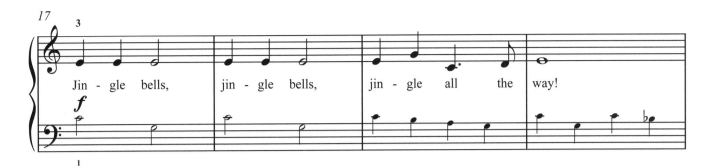

2. A day or two ago I thought I'd take a ride,
and soon Miss Fanny Bright was seated by my side.
The horse was lean and lank,
Misfortune seemed his lot,
he got into a drifted bank and we, we got upsot.
Jingle bells . . .

3. Now the ground is white, go it while you're young;
take the girls tonight, and sing this sleighing song.
Just get a bobtailed bay, two-forty for his speed,
then hitch him to an open sleigh, and crack!
you'll take the lead.
Jingle bells . . .

5. The First Nowell

also known as *The First Noël*

Traditional carol from England
Arr.: Hans-Günter Heumann

Moderato

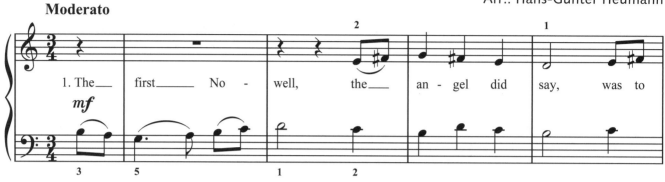

1. The ___ first ___ No - well, the ___ an - gel did say, was to

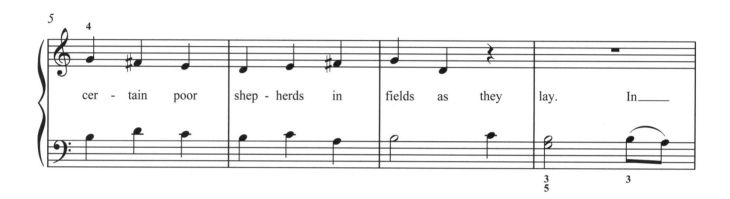

cer - tain poor shep - herds in fields as they lay. In ___

fields ___ where ___ they lay, ___ keep - ing their sheep, on a

cold win - ter's night ___ that was ___ so deep. No -

well,_____ No - well, No - well, No - well.

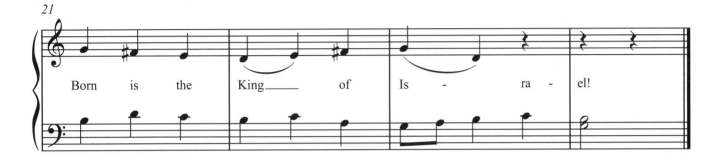

Born is the King_____ of Is - ra - el!

2. They looked up and saw a star,
   shining in the east beyond them far.
   And to the earth it gave great light,
   and so it continued both day and night.
   Nowell, ... etc.

3. And by the light of that same star,
   three wise men came from country far;
   To seek for a king was their intent,
   and to follow the star wherever it went.
   Nowell, ... etc.

4. This star drew nigh to the northwest,
   o'er Bethlehem it took its rest,
   and there it did both stop and stay
   right over the place where Jesus lay.
   Nowell, ... etc.

6. Joy to the World

1st Version: Very easy

Text by Isaac Watts (1674–1748)
Music by George Frideric Handel (1685–1759)
Arr.: Hans-Günter Heumann

Allegro

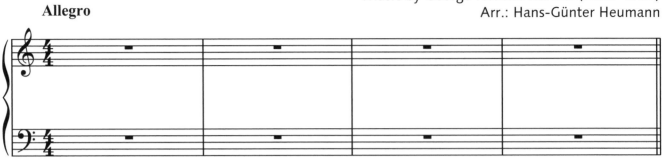

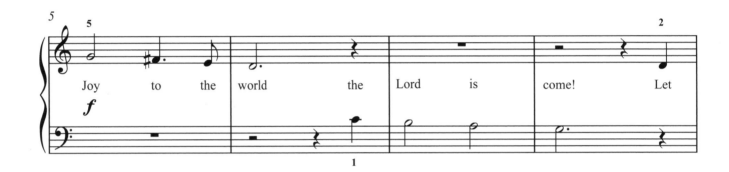

Joy to the world the Lord is come! Let

Accompaniment With accompaniment, student plays one octave higher than written.

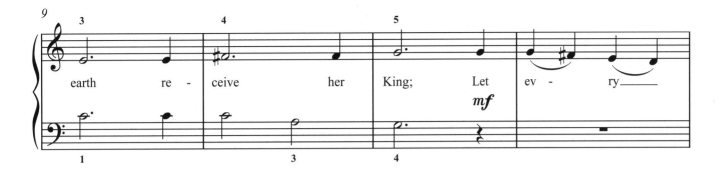

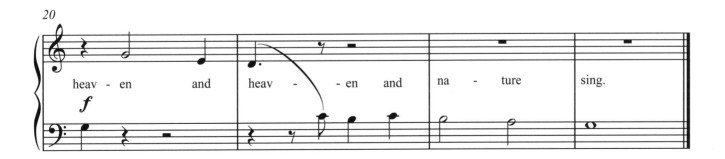

7. Silent Night

1st Version: Very easy

Text by Joseph Mohr (1792–1848)
Music by Franz Xaver Gruber (1787–1863)
Arr.: Hans-Günter Heumann

Accompaniment   With accompaniment, student plays one octave higher than written.

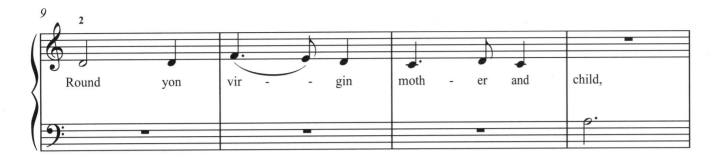

Round   yon   vir - gin   moth - er and   child,

ho - ly   in - fant so   ten - der and   mild.

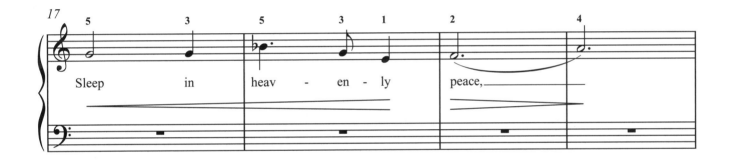

Sleep   in   heav - en - ly   peace,

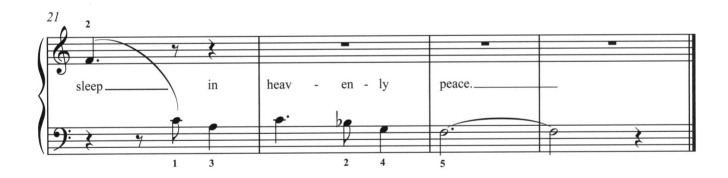

sleep   in   heav - en - ly   peace.

2. Silent night! Holy night!
    Shepherds quake at the sight.
    Glories stream from heaven afar,
    Heavenly host sing Alleluia.
    Christ, the Saviour is born!
    Christ, the Saviour is born!

3. Silent night! Holy night!
    Son of God, love's pure light.
    Radiant beams from thy holy face,
    With the dawn of redeeming grace.
    Jesus, Lord, at thy birth,
    Jesus, Lord, at thy birth.

8. I Saw Three Ships

Benjamin Russell Hanby (1833–1867)
Arr.: Hans-Günter Heumann

Con moto

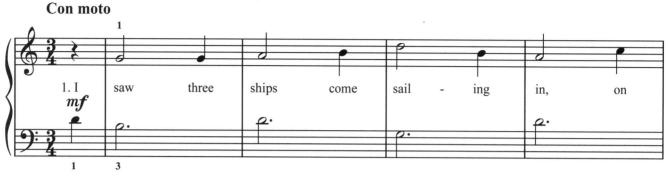

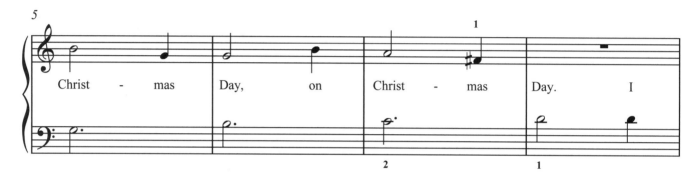

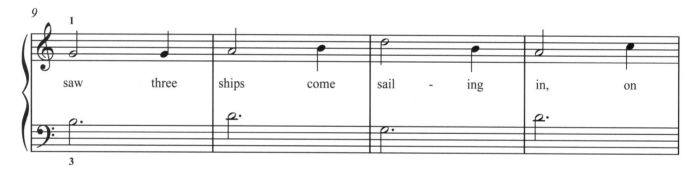

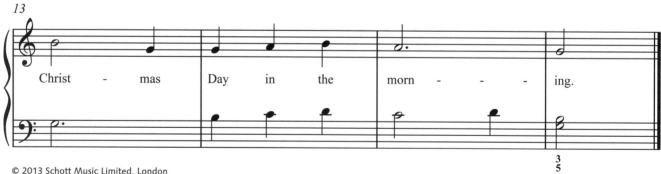

2. And what was in those ships all three,
   on Christmas Day, on Christmas Day?
   And what was in those ships all three,
   on Christmas Day in the morning?

3. The Virgin Mary and Christ were there,
   on Christmas Day, on Christmas Day,
   the Virgin Mary and Christ were there,
   on Christmas Day in the morning.

9. O Christmas Tree

O Tannenbaum

Text by Ernst Anschütz (1780–1861)
Traditional Folk Tune from Germany
Arr.: Hans-Günter Heumann

2. O Christmas tree, o Christmas tree,
   you give us so much pleasure!
   How oft at Christmas tide the sight,
   a green fir tree, gives us delight!
   O Christmas tree, o Christmas tree,
   you give us so much pleasure!

3. O Christmas tree, o Christmas tree,
   forever true your colour.
   Your boughs so green in summertime
   stay bravely green in wintertime.
   O Christmas tree, o Christmas tree,
   forever true your colour.

4. O Christmas tree, o Christmas tree,
   you fill my heart with music.
   Reminding me on Christmas Day
   to think of you and then be gay.
   O Christmas tree, o Christmas tree,
   you fill my heart with music.

10. Up on the Housetop

Benjamin Russell Hanby (1833–1867)
Arr.: Hans-Günter Heumann

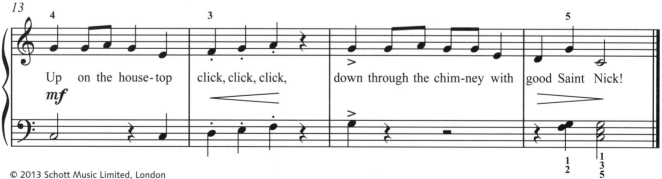

11. Pat-a-Pan

Bernard de la Monnoye (1641–1728)
Arr.: Hans-Günter Heumann

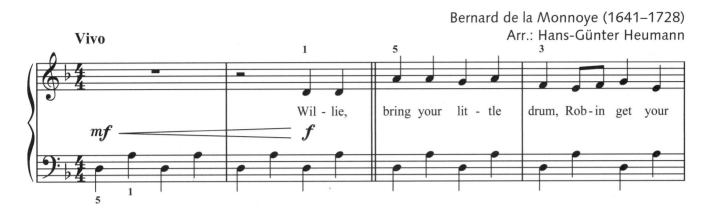

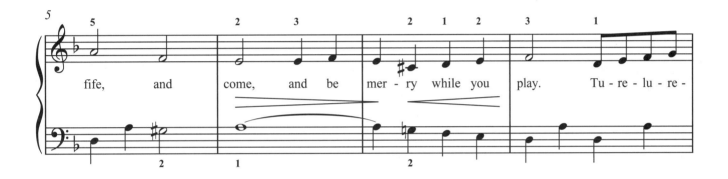

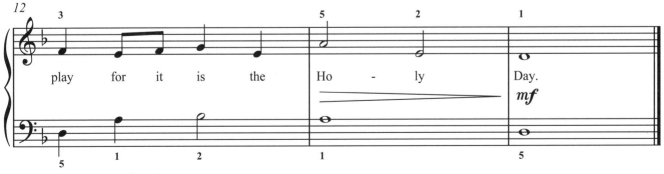

12. Once in Royal David's City

Text by Cecil Francis Alexander (1818–1895)
Music by Henry John Gauntlett (1805–1876)
Arr.: Hans-Günter Heumann

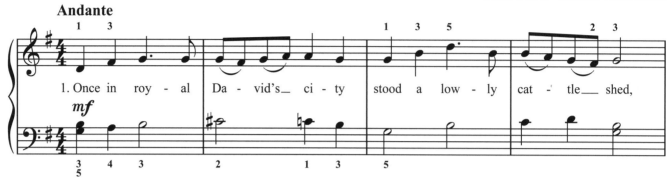

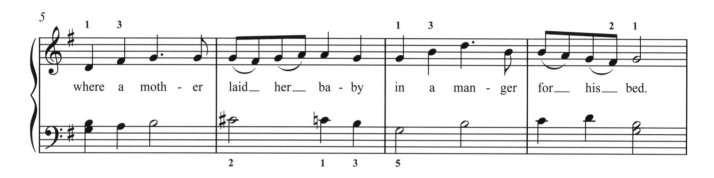

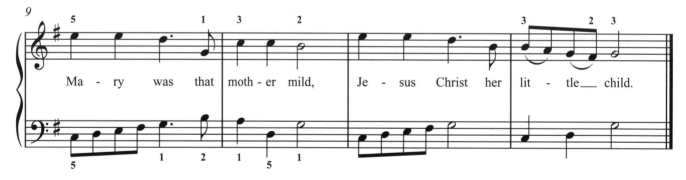

2. He came down to earth from heaven,
   who is God and Lord of all,
   and His shelter was a stable,
   and His cradle was a stall.
   With the poor, and mean, and lowly,
   lived on earth our Saviour holy.

3. And our eyes at last shall see Him,
   through His own redeeming love.
   For that child, so dear and gentle,
   is our Lord in Heaven above.
   And He leads His children on,
   to the place where He is gone.

13. Good King Wenceslas

Text by John Mason Neale (1818–1866)
Music: Traditional English Carol
Arr.: Hans-Günter Heumann

Moderato

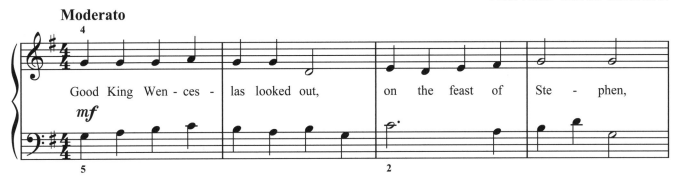

Good King Wen - ces - las looked out, on the feast of Ste - phen,

mf

when the snow lay round a - bout, deep and crisp and ev - en.

Bright - ly shone the moon that night, though the frost was cru - el,

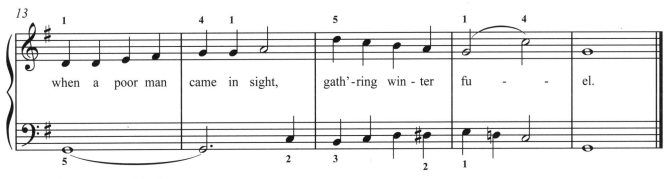

when a poor man came in sight, gath'-ring win - ter fu - el.

14. In dulci jubilo

English Words by Robert Lucas de Pearsall (1795–1856)
Traditional Christmas carol, 14th or 15th century
Arr.: Hans-Günter Heumann

Con moto

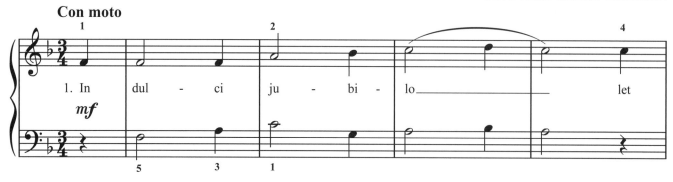

1. In dul - ci ju - bi - lo _____ let

mf

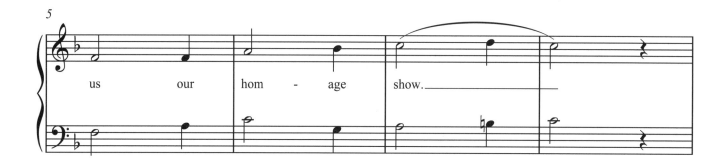

us our hom - age show. _____

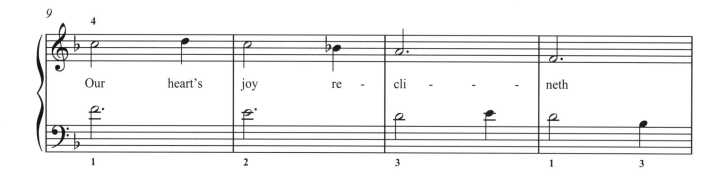

Our heart's joy re - cli - - - neth

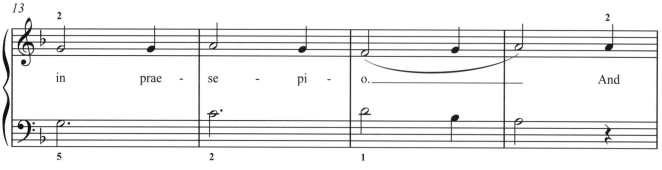

in prae - se - pi - o. _____ And

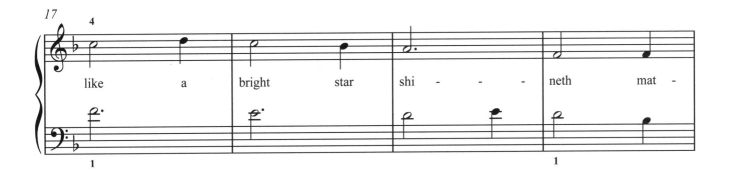

like a bright star shi - - - neth mat -

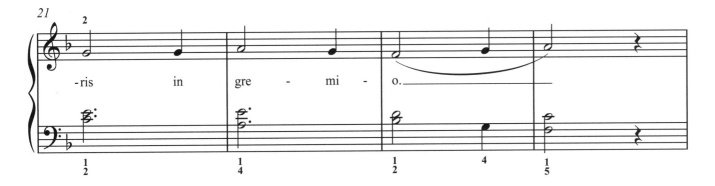

-ris in gre - mi - o.

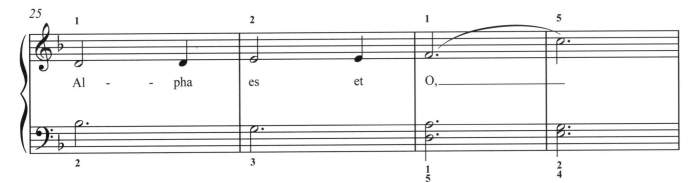

Al - pha es et O,

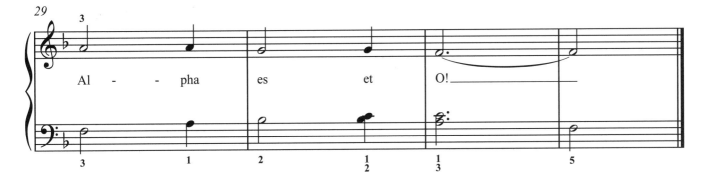

Al - pha es et O!

2. O Jesu parvule! My heart is sore for thee!
   Hear me, I beseech thee, o puer optime!
   My prayer let it reach thee, o princeps gloriae!
   Trahe me post te! Trahe me post te!

3. O patris caritas! O nati lenitas!
   Deep were we stained, per nostra criminal.
   But thou has for us gained, coelorum gaudia:
   O that we were there, o that we were there!

15. We Three Kings of Orient Are

John Henry Hopkins (1820–1891)
Arr.: Hans-Günter Heumann

star with roy - al beau - ty bright,

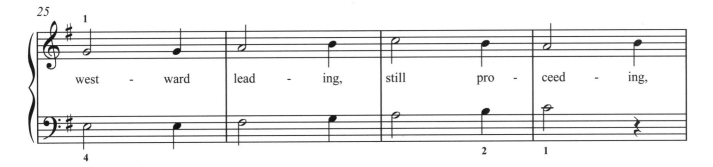

west - ward lead - ing, still pro - ceed - ing,

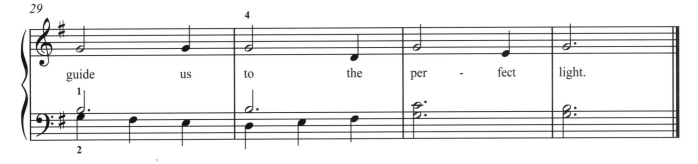

guide us to the per - fect light.

2. Born a King on Bethlehem's plain,
   gold I bring to crown Him again;
   King forever, ceasing never
   over us all to reign.
   O, star of wonder, ... etc.

3. Frankincense to offer have I;
   Incense owns a Deity nigh,
   prayer and praising all men raising,
   worship Him, God on high.
   O, star of wonder, ... etc.

4. Myrrh is mine, its bitter perfume,
   breathes a life of gathering gloom,
   sorrowing, sighing, bleeding, dying,
   sealed in the stone-cold tomb.
   O, star of wonder, ... etc.

5. Glorious now, behold Him arise,
   King and God and Sacrifice;
   Heaven sings "Hallelujah!"
   "Hallelujah!" earth replies.
   O, star of wonder, ... etc.

16. The Coventry Carol

Traditional carol from England, 16th century
Arr.: Hans-Günter Heumann

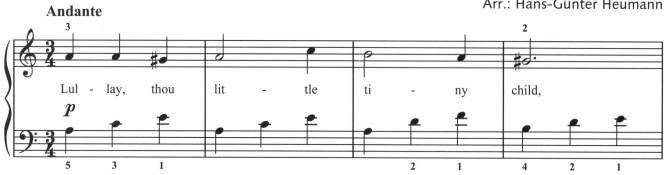

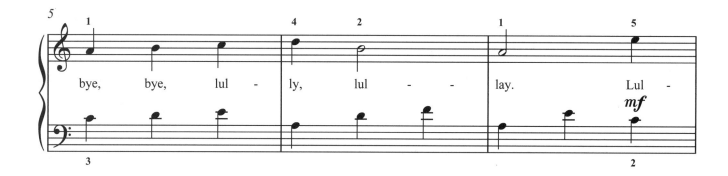

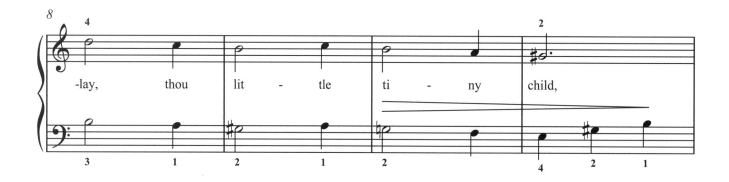

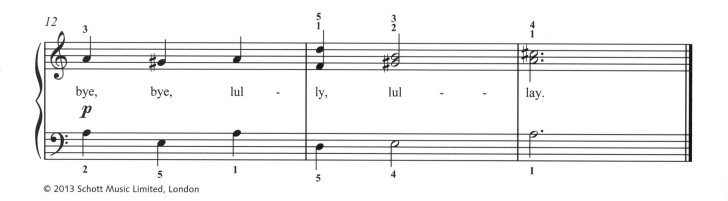

17. The Holly and the Ivy

Traditional carol from England
Arr.: Hans-Günter Heumann

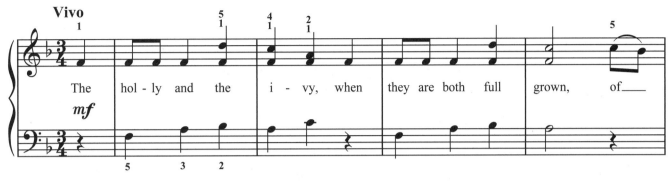

The hol-ly and the i - vy, when they are both full grown, of___

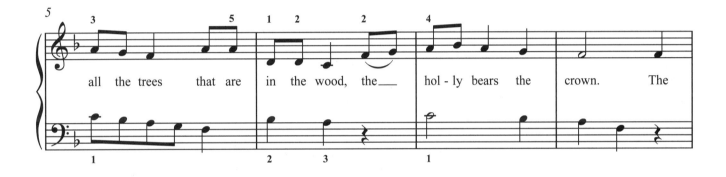

all the trees that are in the wood, the___ hol - ly bears the crown. The

ris - ing of the sun,___ and the run-ning of the deer, the___

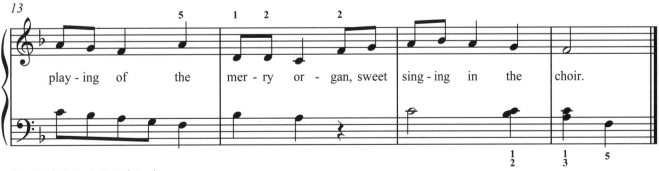

play-ing of the mer - ry or - gan, sweet sing - ing in the choir.

18. Silent Night

2nd Version: Easy

Text by Joseph Mohr (1792–1848)
Music by Franz Xaver Gruber (1787–1863)
Arr.: Hans-Günter Heumann

1. Si - lent night! Ho - ly night!

All is calm, all is bright.

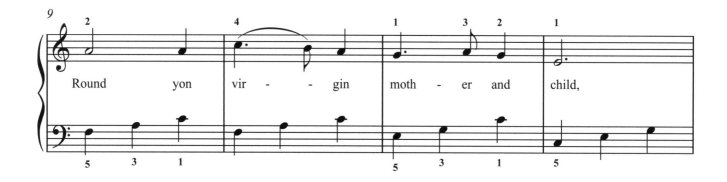

Round yon vir - gin moth - er and child,

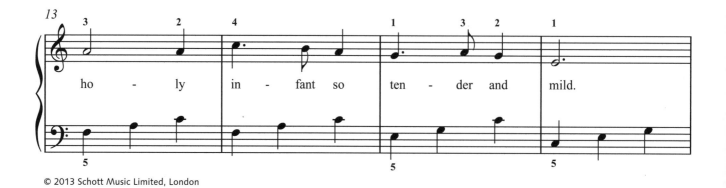

ho - ly in - fant so ten - der and mild.

2. Silent night! Holy night!
   Shepherds quake at the sight.
   Glories stream from heaven afar,
   heavenly hosts sing Alleluia!
   Christ the saviour is born,
   Christ the saviour is born.

3. Silent night! Holy night!
   Son of God, love's pure light.
   Radiant beams from thy holy face,
   with the dawn of redeeming grace.
   Jesus, Lord, at thy birth,
   Jesus, Lord, at thy birth.

19. Joy to the World

2nd Version: Easy

Text by Isaac Watts (1674–1748)
Music by George Frideric Handel (1685–1759)
Arr.: Hans-Günter Heumann

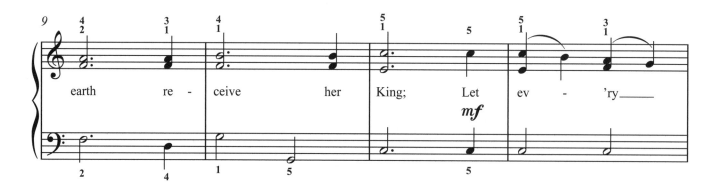

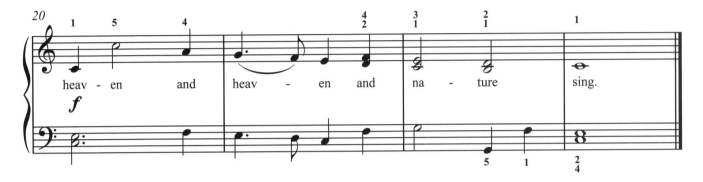

2. Joy to the earth, the Saviour reigns!
   Your sweetest songs employ;
   While fields and streams and hills and plains
   repeat the sounding joy,
   repeat the sounding joy,
   repeat, repeat the sounding joy.

3. No more let sins and sorrows grow,
   nor thorns infest the ground;
   He comes to make His blessings flow
   far as the curse is found,
   far as the curse is found,
   far as, far as the curse is found.

4. He rules the world with truth and grace,
   and makes the nations prove.
   The glories of His righteousness,
   the wonders of His love,
   the wonders of His love,
   the wonders, wonders of His love.

20. It Came Upon the Midnight Clear

Text by Edmund Sears (1810–1876)
Music by Richard Storrs Willis (1819–1900)
Arr.: Hans-Günter Heumann

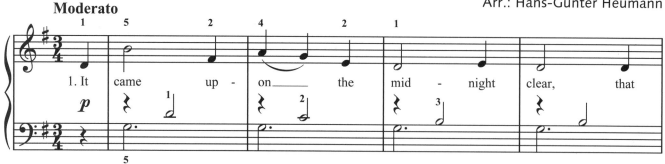

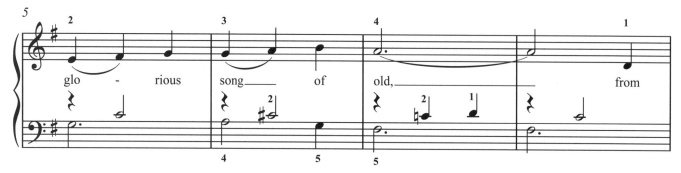

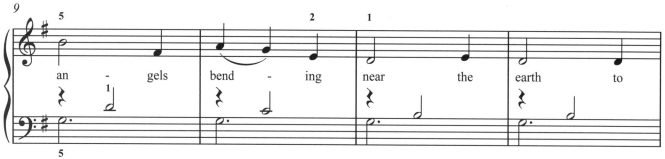

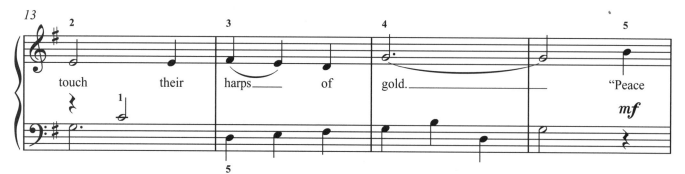

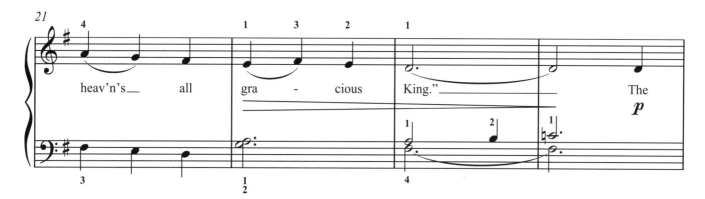

heav'n's___ all gra - cious King."___ The *p*

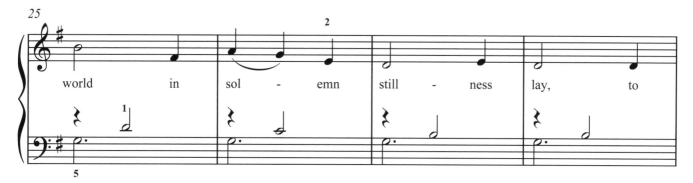

world in sol - emn still - ness lay, to

hear the an - - gels sing.___

2. Still through the cloven skies they come,
   with peaceful wings unfurled,
   and still their heavenly music floats
   o'er all the weary world.
   Above its sad and lowly plains
   they bend on hovering wing,
   and ever o'er its Babel sounds
   the blessed angels sing.

3. O ye, beneath life's crushing load,
   whose forms are bending low.
   Who toil along the climbing way
   with painful steps and slow.
   Look now, for glad and golden hours
   come swiftly on the wing,
   o rest beside the weary road
   and hear the angels sing.

4. For lo! the days are hastening on,
   by prophets seen of old,
   when with the ever-circling years
   shall come the time foretold.
   When the new heaven and earth shall own
   the Prince of Peace, their King,
   and the whole world send back the song
   which now the angels sing.

21. Away in a Manger

Mueller (1887)

Text: Anonymous
Music by James Ramsey Murray (1841–1905)
Arr.: Hans-Günter Heumann

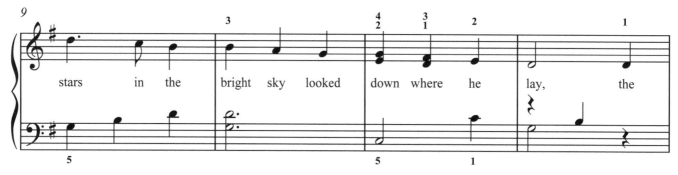

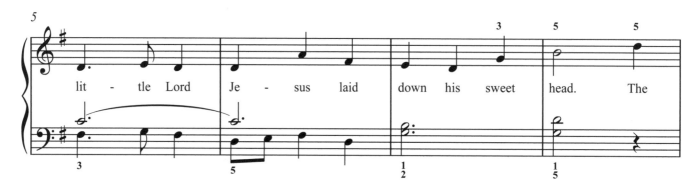

2. The cattle are lowing, the baby awakes,
   but little Lord Jesus no crying he makes.
   I love thee, Lord Jesus, look down from the sky,
   and stay by my side until morning is nigh.

3. Be near me, Lord Jesus, I ask thee to stay
   close by me forever, and love me, I pray.
   Bless all the dear children in thy tender care,
   and fit us for heaven, to live with thee there.

22. Away in a Manger

Cradle Song (1895)

Text: Anonymous
Music by William James Kirkpatrick (1838–1921)
Arr.: Hans-Günter Heumann

2. The cattle are lowing, the baby awakes,
   but little Lord Jesus no crying he makes.
   I love thee, Lord Jesus, look down from the sky,
   and stay by my side until morning is nigh.

3. Be near me, Lord Jesus, I ask thee to stay
   close by me forever, and love me, I pray.
   Bless all the dear children in thy tender care,
   and fit us for heaven, to live with thee there.

23. Angels from the Realms of Glory

Gloria in excelsis Deo

Text by James Montgomery (1771–1854)
Traditional French carol
Arr.: Hans-Günter Heumann

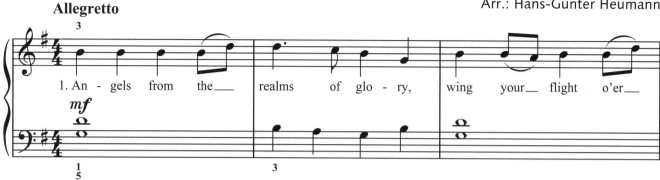

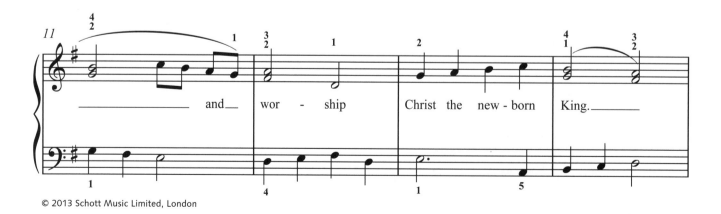

Come_____ and__

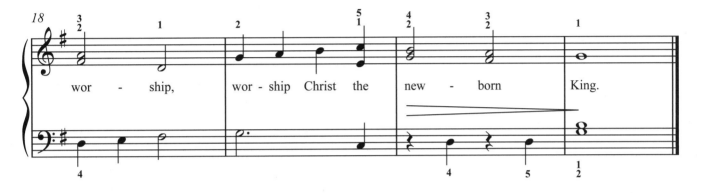

wor - ship, wor - ship Christ the new - born King.

2. Shepherds in the fields abiding,
   watching o'er your flocks by night.
   God with us is now residing,
   yonder shines the infant light.
   Come ... etc.

3. Sages leave your contemplations,
   brighter visions beam afar.
   Seek the great Desire of nations,
   ye have seen His natal star.
   Come ... etc.

4. Though in infant now we view him,
   he shall fill Father's throne.
   Gather all the nations to Him,
   every knee shall then bow down.
   Come ... etc.

5. All creation, join in praising,
   God, the Father, Spirit, Son.
   Evermore your voices raising
   to th'eternal Three in One.
   Come ... etc.

38

24. Deck the Hall

Traditional New Year's Eve carol from Wales
Arr.: Hans-Günter Heumann

© 2013 Schott Music Limited, London

2. See the blazing yule before us,
   fa-la-la-la-la, la-la-la-la.
   Strike the harp and join the chorus,
   fa-la-la-la-la, la-la-la-la.
   Follow me in merry measure,
   fa-la-la, la-la-la, la-la-la.
   While I tell of Christmas treasure,
   fa-la-la-la-la, la-la-la-la.

3. Fast away the old year passes,
   fa-la-la-la-la, la-la-la-la.
   Hail the new, ye lads and lasses,
   fa-la-la-la-la, la-la-la-la.
   Sing we joyous all together,
   fa-la-la, la-la-la, la-la-la.
   Heedless of the wind and weather,
   fa-la-la-la-la, la-la-la-la.

25. O Little Town of Bethlehem

Text by Phillips Brooks (1835–1893)
Music by Lewis Redner (1831–1908)
Arr.: Hans-Günter Heumann

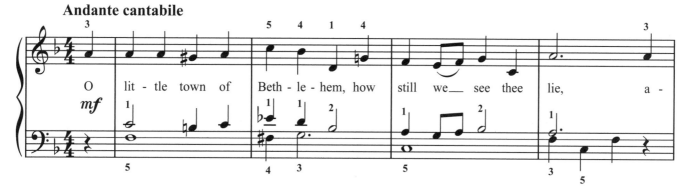

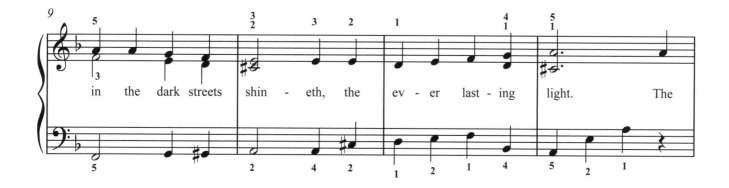

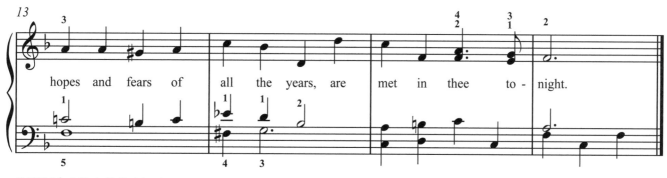

26. Dance of the Sugar Plum Fairy

from the ballet *The Nutcracker*

Pyotr Ilyich Tchaikovsky (1840–1893)

Arr.: Hans-Günter Heumann

Andante non troppo ♩ = 108

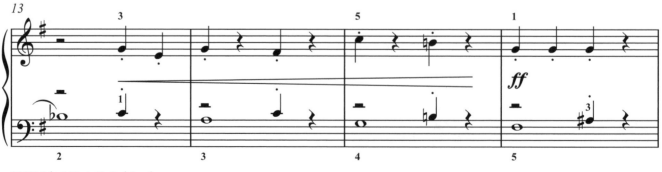

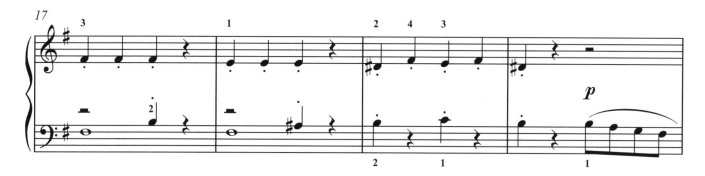
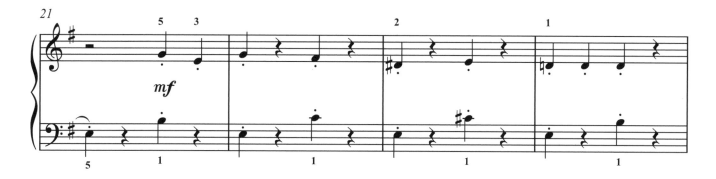
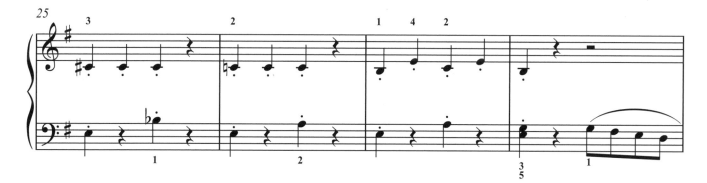
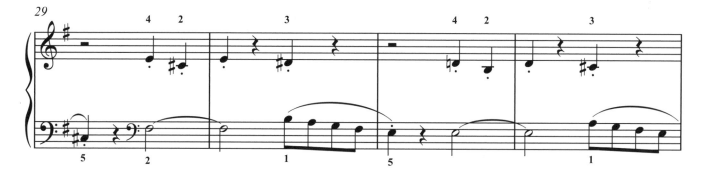
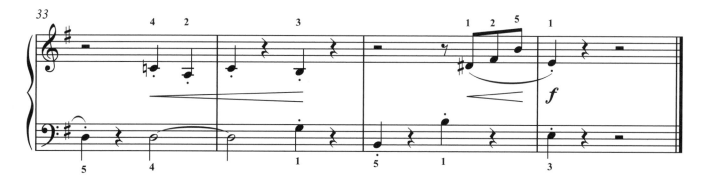

27. God Rest You Merry, Gentlemen

also known as *God Rest Ye Merry, Gentlemen*

Traditional carol from England
Arr.: Hans-Günter Heumann

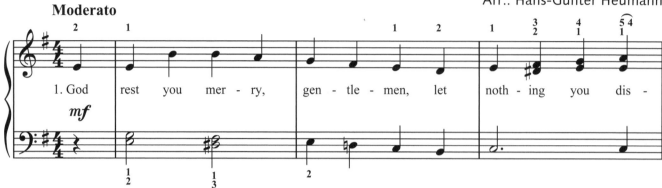

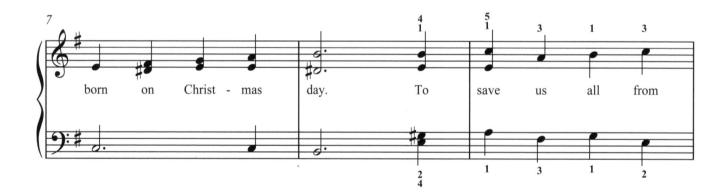

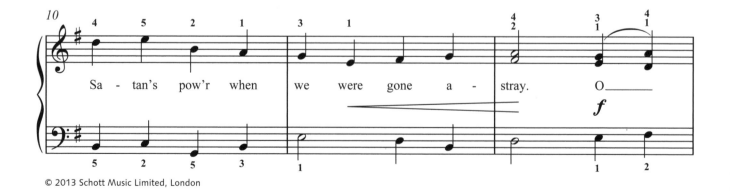

ti - dings of com - fort and joy, com - fort and

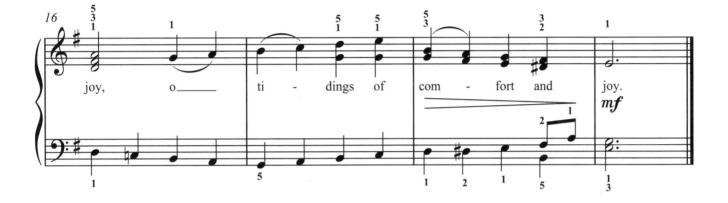

joy, o_____ ti - dings of com - fort and joy.

mf

2. From God our heavenly Father,
   a blessed angel came,
   and unto certain shepherds
   brought tidings of the same,
   how that in Bethlehem was born
   the Son of God by name,
   o, tidings of comfort and joy,
   comfort and joy,
   o, tidings of comfort and joy.

3. "Fear not, then," said the angel,
   "let nothing you affright,
   this day is born a Saviour
   of pure Virgin bright,
   o free all those who trust in Him
   from Satan's power and might."
   O, tidings of comfort and joy,
   comfort and joy,
   o, tidings of comfort and joy.

28. Go, Tell It on the Mountain

Traditional Spiritual
Arr.: Hans-Günter Heumann

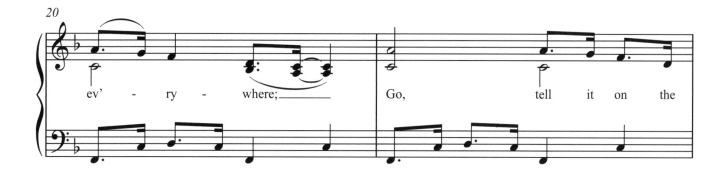

2. When I was a sinner
   I prayed both night and day.
   I asked the Lord to help me
   and He showed me the way.

3. He made me a watchman
   upon the city wall,
   and if I am a Christian
   I am the least of all.

29. Hark! The Herald Angels Sing

Text by Charles Wesley (1707–1788)
Music by Felix Mendelssohn Bartholdy (1809–1847)
Arr.: Hans-Günter Heumann

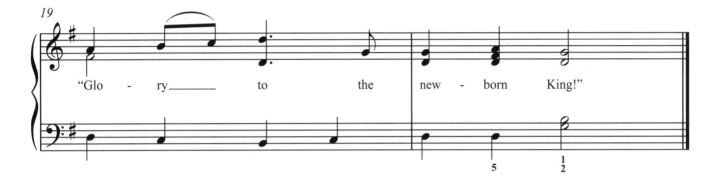

2. Christ, by highest heaven adored,
Christ, the everlasting Lord;
Late in time behold Him come,
offspring of the Virgin's womb.
Veiled in flesh the godhead see
hail, th'incarnate Deity!
Pleased as man with man to dwell,
Jesus our Emmanuel.
Hark! The herald angels sing:
"Glory to the newborn King!"

3. Hail, the heaven-born Prince of Peace!
Hail, the Sun of Righteousness!
Light and life to all He brings,
risen with healing in his wings.
Mild He lays His glory by,
born that man no more may die,
born to raise the sons of earth,
born to give them second birth.
Hark! The herald angels sing:
"Glory to the newborn King!"

30. Hallelujah

from the oratorio *Messiah*

George Frideric Handel (1685–1759)

Arr.: Hans-Günter Heumann

Allegro moderato 𝅗𝅥 = 100

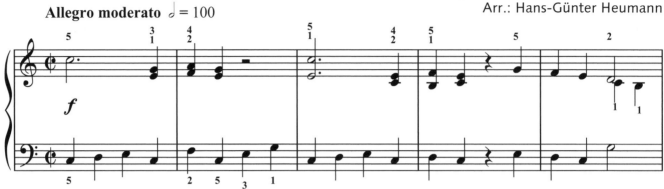

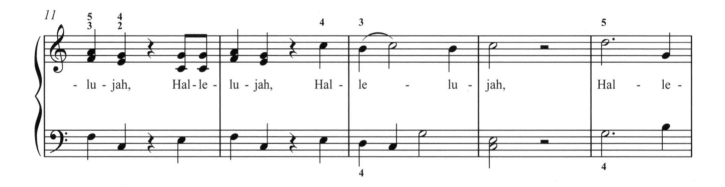

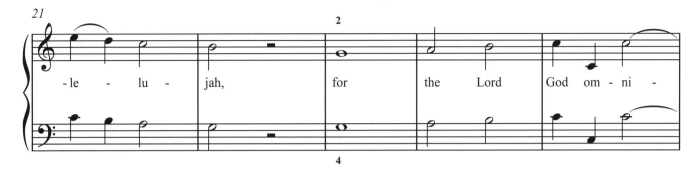

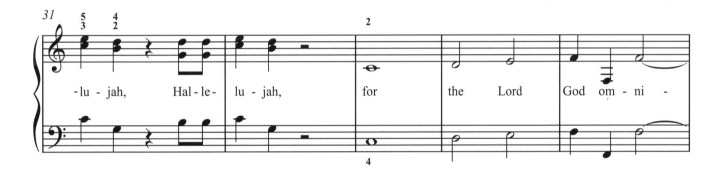

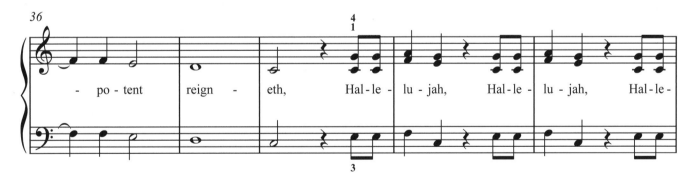

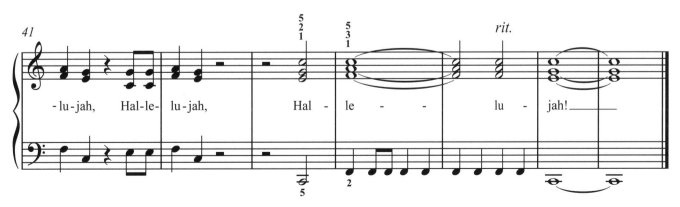

31. The Skaters

Les Patineurs, from Op. 183, No. 1

Émile Waldteufel (1837–1915)
Arr.: Hans-Günter Heumann

Tempo di Valse ♩. = 60

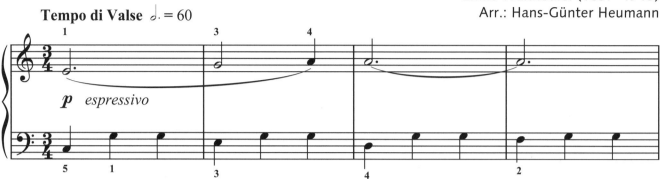

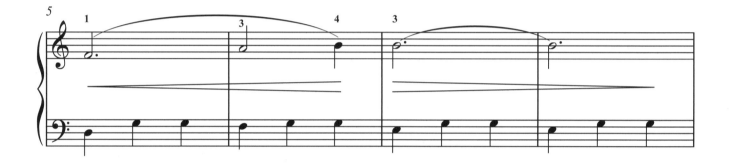

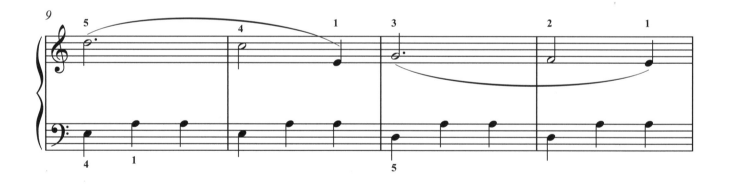

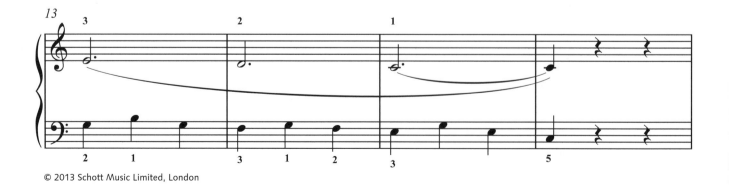

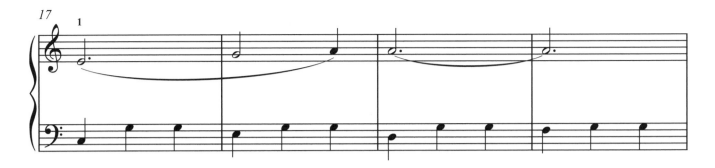

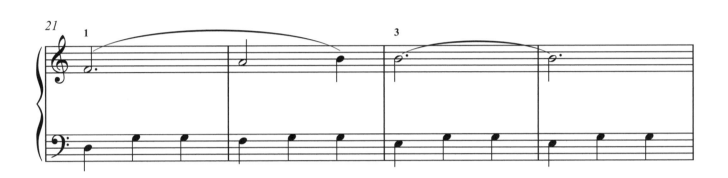

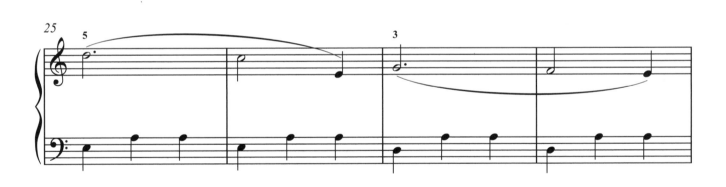

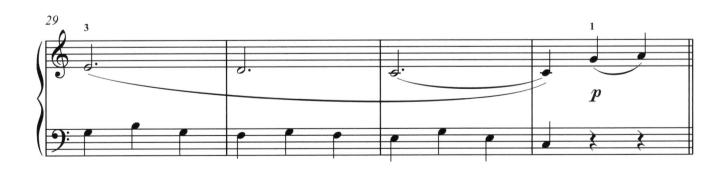

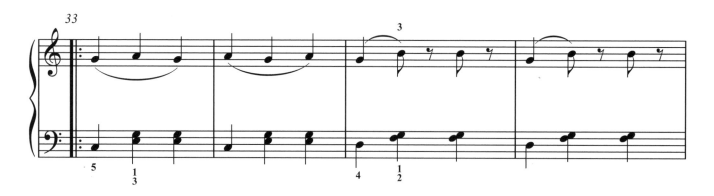

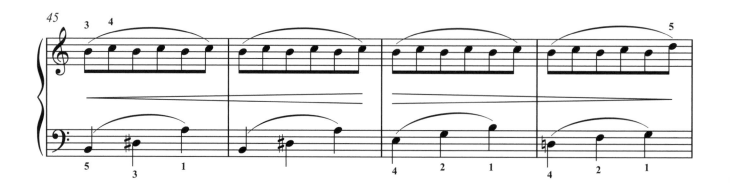

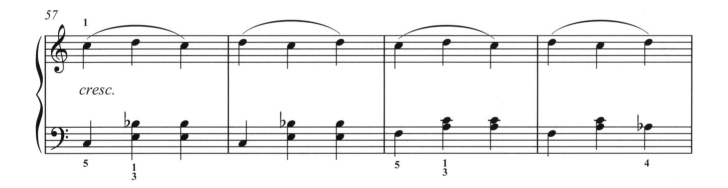

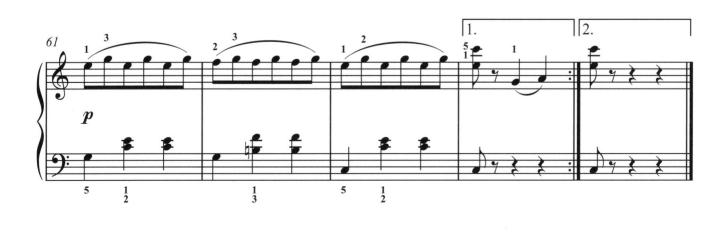

32. Shepherd's Music

Sinfonia from *Christmas Oratorio* BWV 248

Johann Sebastian Bach (1685–1750)
Arr.: Hans-Günter Heumann

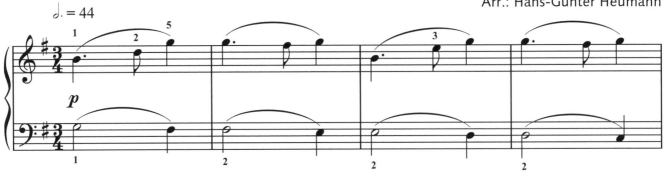

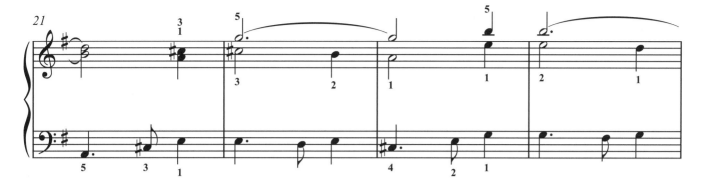

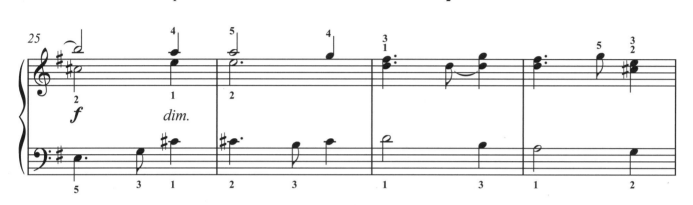

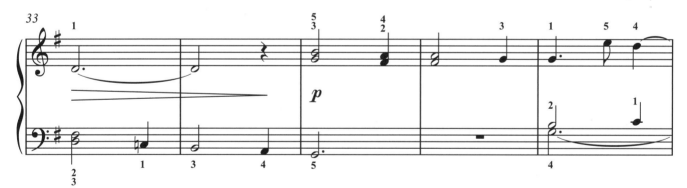

33. The Petersburg Sleigh Ride

Theme from Op. 57

Richard Eilenberg (1848–1927)
Arr.: Hans-Günter Heumann

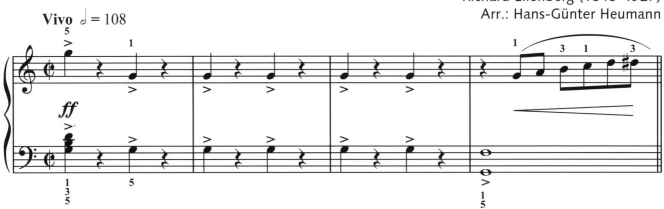

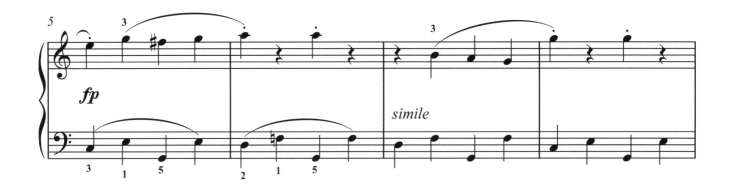

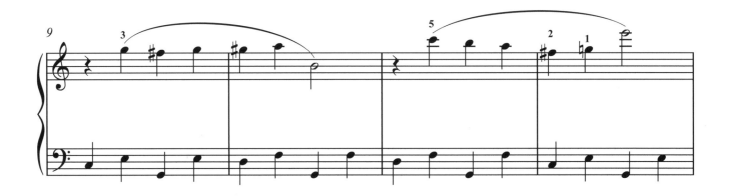

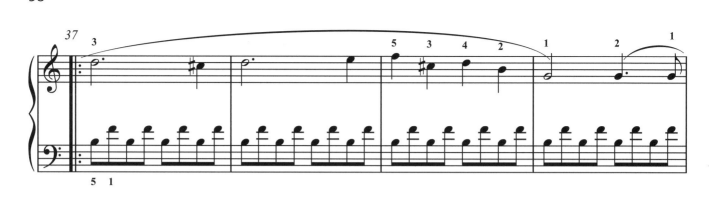

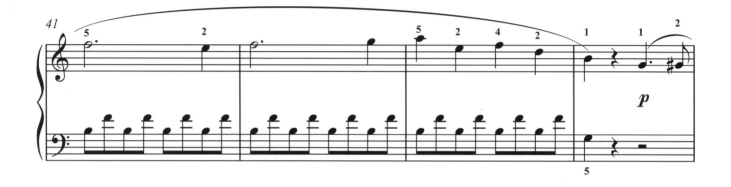

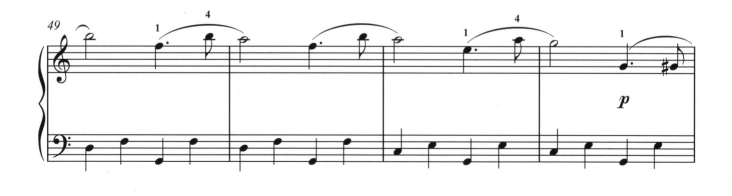

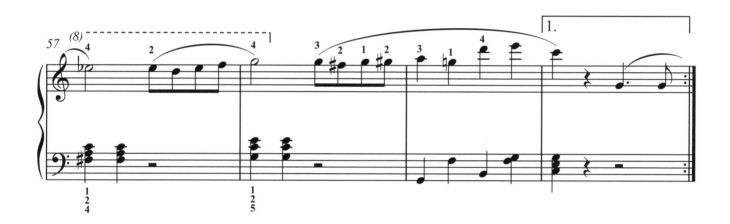

34. Winter Time

from *Album for the Young* Op. 68, No. 38

Robert Schumann (1810–1856)
Arr.: Hans-Günter Heumann

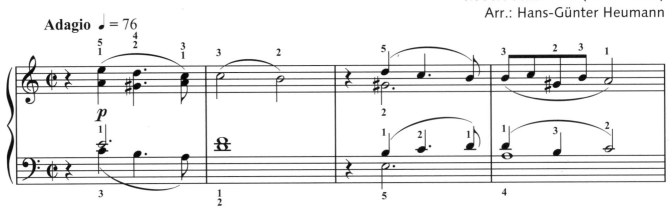

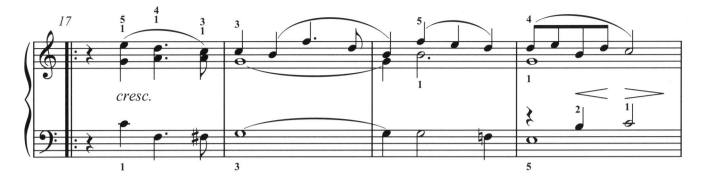

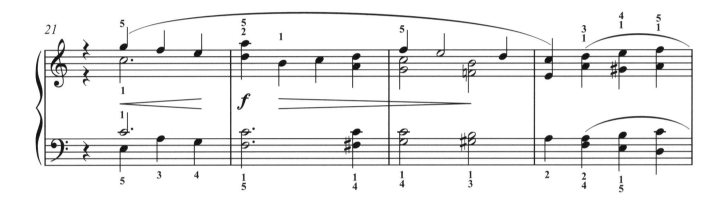

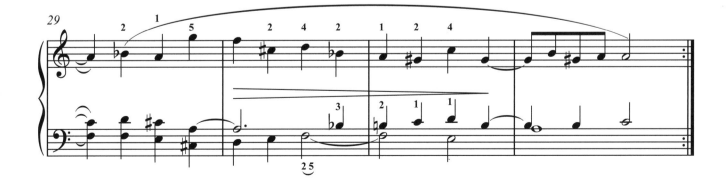

35. Christmas

December from the *Seasons* Op. 37/2, No. 12

Pyotr Ilyich Tchaikovsky (1840–1893)
Arr.: Hans-Günter Heumann

Tempo di Valse ♩. = 60

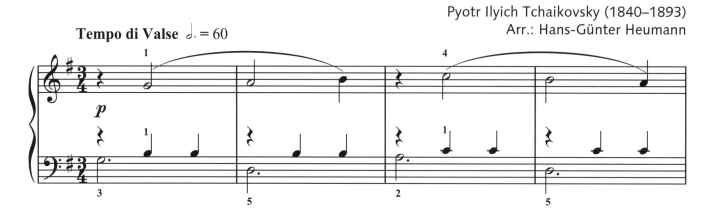

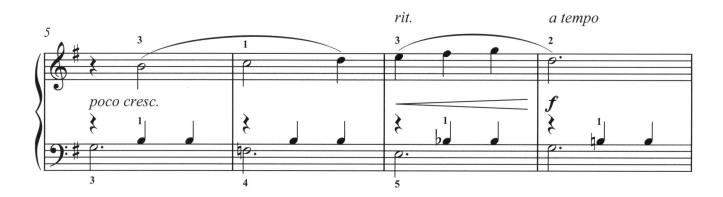

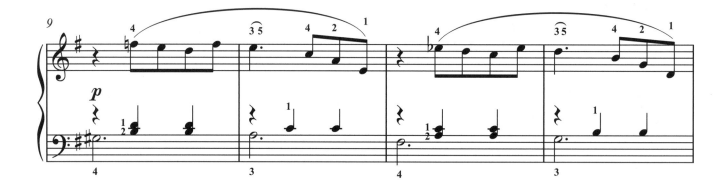

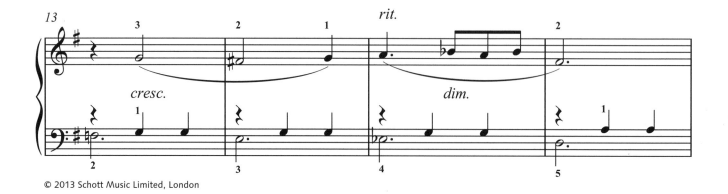

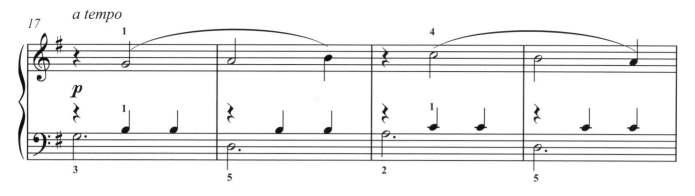

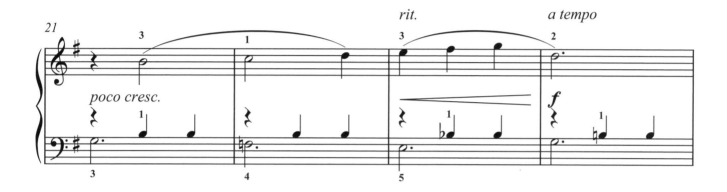